MYSTERIES
OF THE ANCIENT WORLD

THE EXTINCTION OF
THE DINOSAURS

£1·99

Douglas Palmer

WEIDENFELD & NICOLSON
LONDON

The word 'dinosaur' has something of a double meaning, there is the metaphorical dinosaur, the 'has been' . . . 'consigned to the dustbin of history' and then there are the 'dinosaurs' of *Jurassic Park*, beloved by children of all ages. These dinosaurs are either seemingly benign plant-eaters, or 'bad guys', red-eyed, ravenous meat-eating predators. Why, of all the groups of animals and plants that have become extinct over the last 600 million years and more of life on Earth, should the dinosaurs have acquired this image? Part of the explanation is that when the dinosaurs were invented in the 19th century, they inherited the mantle of the dragons of myth and folklore. Since then the image of the dinosaurs has gone through a number of transformations which have kept them in fashion.

Helpless herbivores may have replaced maidens in distress, but the killer image of the dragon/dinosaur retains its power.

The remains of these mysterious animals combine immensity of size with the curiously inexpressive, staring creepiness of reptiles. How much truth is there behind this image? What were these dinosaurs really like? Does their rise and fall justify their status as an object lesson in why not to overdo things and become a victim of your own success?

In late Permian times, some 230 million years before humans appeared on Earth, a group of scaly-skinned, egg-laying reptiles evolved and gradually came to dominate the planet. For over 155 million years, these now-extinct reptiles, which came to be known as dinosaurs, ruled the landscapes of the world from Alaska to Antarctica. In the history of life, no other group of animals has been so successful for so long. So far, mammals have only been in charge for a mere 65 million years. One of the great mysteries of the dinosaurs is why, if they were so successful, did they die out 65 million years ago? Why should the dinosaurs have been 'deselected', while other reptiles, such as terrestrial crocodiles and lizards and aquatic turtles, survived and prospered? Did they fall because they were unable to adapt and change, or were they blasted off by a meteorite? Did it all end with a whimper or a bang?

Until the end of the 18th century the Old Testament view of creation was the prevailing one, and the world was believed to be 6,000 years old. The history and evolution of life on Earth that is accepted today was not discovered until the 19th century, and one of the greatest and most surprising scientific discoveries of 19th-century science was that of the extinct fossil reptiles, especially the dinosaurs.

Not so terrible. The only model for the dinosaurs available to the Victorian scientists were the plant-eating Iguana lizards.

The First Discoveries

Before the dinosaurs were 'invented' the first intimation that the world had once been populated by weird and wonderful animals that no longer existed was provided by the discovery in 1786 of an enormous skull with metre-long jaws, armed with ferocious teeth in a chalk quarry in Maastricht, Netherlands. Scientists could not agree on what kind of animal it had been, for it looked like a cross between a crocodile and toothed whale, so it was reconstructed as a

***B**east of Maastricht: the 1786 discovery of enormous reptilian fossil jaws provided the first evidence that extinction had occurred.*

extinction had not yet been thought of. Such was the Beast of Maastricht's

crocodile-like animal. Although no such animal was known at the time, it was still possible that such an animal might exist somewhere on Earth:

fame that in 1795, it was captured by Napoleon's army and exhibited in Paris.

Some of the most important early finds of ancient monsters were made at the very beginning of the 19th century. They were found by a Dorset woman,

ICHTHYOSAURUS COMMUNIS, Conybeare.

*S*he sold sea-
shells: Mary
Anning discovered
some of the first
fossil reptiles and
earned her living
by selling them to
scientists.

The first real fossil monsters to excite public interest were the marine reptiles discovered in England early in the 19th century. Mary Anning, and her family in the 200-million-year-old rocks of Lyme Regis in Dorset. The family eked out a precarious existence scouring the limestone cliffs for fossils to sell to growing numbers of tourists who came to admire the wild seascape and its 'quaint native' inhabitants.

Between 1811 and 1830 the Annings uncovered complete flattened skeletons of creatures up to 4 m long, which had toothed beaks like mammalian dolphins mixed with other, predominantly reptilian characteristics. These ichthyosaurs (meaning fish-lizards) and plesiosaurs (near-lizards) had evidently lived in ancient seas, because they were found with the shells of typically marine clams, starfish and squid-like cephalopods. The likelihood of extinction was becoming more acceptable, but the question of how and when it occurred was still highly contentious. After all, as recorded in the Bible, the Flood could well have been responsible for drowning all these fossil creatures found in the rocks.

Eminent scientists of the day visited the Annings' little fossil shop and bought specimens for the growing collections of the university museums of Cambridge and Oxford and the national collection in London. They were the

9

first 'fossil dragons' to stir the public imagination – even the King of Saxony visited Mary to admire the results of her labours – and the first large extinct animals to be illustrated in reconstructions of their living environments. These early-Victorian illustrations provided the model for today's cryptic beasts, such as the Loch Ness 'monster'.

In 1825 some mysterious fossil bones were found near Cuckfield, Sussex. The fossils included a few peculiar leaf-shaped teeth with serrated edges and a

*P*uzzling bones: in the 1820s Doctor Gideon Mantell struggled to identify fossil bones from a quarry in Sussex.

*F*rom jumbled bones on this rock slab Mantell attempted to reconstruct Iguanodon, one of the first dinosaurs.

jumble of bones, including a single conical spike or horn-shaped bone about 15 cm long. The local doctor and naturalist, Gideon Mantell, was puzzled. However, it was clear that here was a land-living reptile of several metres size.

The only models scientists had to go on were the living four-legged reptiles – the lizards and crocodiles. Mantell's reconstruction of the animal seems to owe as much to the myth and imagery of St George, and was a distinctly dragon-like beast,

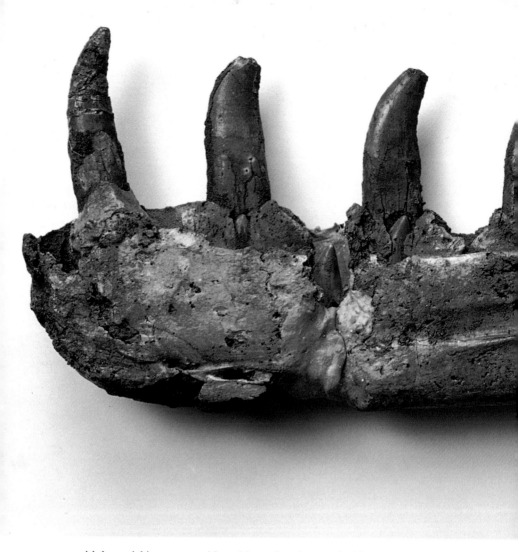

with legs sticking out on either side, rather than tucked in below the bulk of the body as seen in mammals. He placed the spike, rhinoceros-like, on the end of its nose.

Inventing Dinosaurs

Dinosaurs were not 'invented' until 1842, when a British scientist, Richard Owen, first coined the name 'Dinosauria', meaning 'terrible lizard', to distin-

*F*irst meat-
eater: a
jawbone from
Oxford with
flesh-cutting
teeth was given
the name
Megalosaurus
(meaning giant
lizard) in 1822.

guish the recently named fossils *Iguanodon*, *Hylaeosaurus* and *Megalosaurus* from the known living reptiles. Owen calculated that his dinosaurs might be as much as six times the size of an elephant, but that was before 'dinoflation' set in. Little did he know at the time exactly what sort of monster he was creating. His creation was to become a universal icon, eclipsing dragons and even outshining Mary Shelley's monstrous Frankenstein.

The relocation of Joseph Paxton's Crystal Palace from Kensington to

*T*his early view of *Cretaceous dinosaurs shows a curiously inanimate fight between* **Iguanodon** *and* **Megalosaurus.**

*R*ichard Owen *'invented' dinosaurs in 1842 when he grouped the* **Iguanodon, Megalosaurus** *and* **Hylaeosaurus** *in the Order* **Dinosauria.**

*E*pitomizing the cumbersome might of Victorian England, Hawkins's lifesize dinosaurs were an instant crowd-puller at the Crystal Palace.

Sydenham gave Owen a golden opportunity to recreate his concept of the dinosaur in the form of life-size models set in appropriate landscape

To celebrate the first lifesize dinosaur reconstruction, a celebratory meal was held within the Iguanodon model in 1854.

and vegetation. Owen supervised the modelling by Benjamin Waterhouse Hawkins, and the opening by Queen Victoria drew crowds of thousands. The first theme park in the world was open.

*U*nder
Richard
Owen's
instruction,
Waterhouse
Hawkins drew
and modelled
the first
dinosaurs as
heavyweight
rhinoceros-like
lizards.

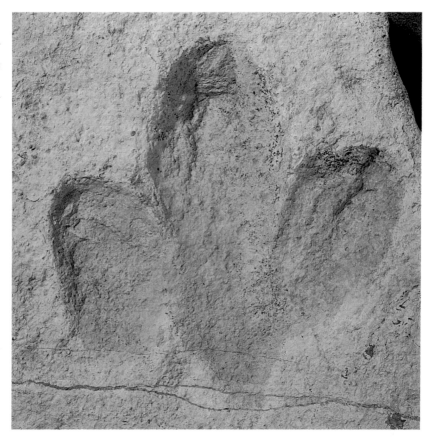

News of the venture soon spread and Hawkins was invited to repeat his success in New York's Central Park. He set about producing an even more ambitious

In the early 19th century the curious three-toed footprints of dinosaurs like **Iguanodon** *were mistaken for those of giant birds.*

scheme with many more reconstructions. Unfortunately, this fell foul of local politics and some of the completed models are reputed to have been broken up and buried in the park (despite searches no remains have been discovered). However, the impetus for dinosaur research had taken off in America in a big way and the whole concept of the dinosaur was to change radically.

The new American image owed its birth to a discovery in 1802, when an

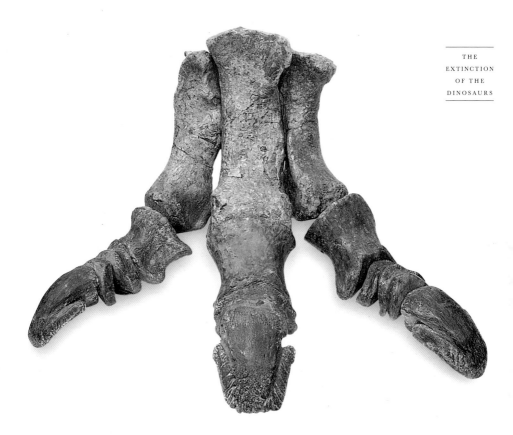

E ven dinosaurs suffered from arthritis in old age, as frilled growths on the toe-bones of this large Iguanodon show.

observant youth by the name of Pliny Moody uncovered some fossil footprints while ploughing on the family farm in Massachusetts. A local naturalist, Edward Hitchcock, eventually described the prints in 1836, and went on to make an impressive collection of other fossil tracks from the red sandstone of a Connecticut valley.

The distinctive and puzzling feature of the tracks was that they had been made by large three-toed animals. At the time, the only creatures known to produce such tracks were birds, so not unreasonably Hitchcock concluded that they must have been made by giant birds. But what he had found were actually dinosaur footprints and so these fossil tracks provided the first evidence that not all dinosaurs were four-legged, as everyone had assumed.

The study of fossil tracks has really taken off in recent years, with amazing finds ranging from the enormous prints of individual sauropods to multiple trackways showing that many dinosaurs were social animals. The plant-eaters formed herds for mutual protection, just as elephants do today, and some of the small carnivores probably hunted in packs or family groups, like lions and hyenas.

In 1858, Joseph Leidy found a partial skeleton in New Jersey, which he reconstructed in a two-legged kangaroo-like posture; but the hunt moved west and really began to take off in the 1870s. Two schoolmasters, Arthur Lakes and O. W. Lucas, independently found dinosaur fossils in Colorado and sent their finds to experts back east.

The first intimation that the hunters were on to something big came in the 1880s when Othneil Marsh of Yale produced the first reconstruction of a sauropod, which he called *Brontosaurus*, meaning 'thunder lizard'. Marsh was somewhat cavalier when he first cobbled together his *Brontosaurus* reconstruction in 1883, for it included the limb-bones and skull of *Camarasaurus*, a quite different animal, and scientists no longer use the name *Brontosaurus*.

With individual limb-bones over a metre long and what seemed like endless vertebrae, it was clear that once upon a time there had been land-living dinosaurs that were by far the largest animals to have lived on land. The unforgettable image of giant plant-eating sauropods over 20 m long and weighing more than 20 tonnes, supported by elephantine pillar-like legs, had invaded the

*D**inosaur graveyard: the discovery in America of abundant dinosaur fossils in the late 19th century revolutionized ideas on how they looked.***

public conscience. Indeed, the bulk of these creatures was so great that it was thought they must have primarily water-dwellers like the hippopotamus.

These dinosaur giants were so impressive that their remains were sought the world over. One of the finest discoveries was the 1907 find of a 22 m long *Brachiosaurus* in East Africa. Its nostrils were right on top of its head, which seemed to support the idea that these giants were aquatic. Now it is realized that *Bra-*

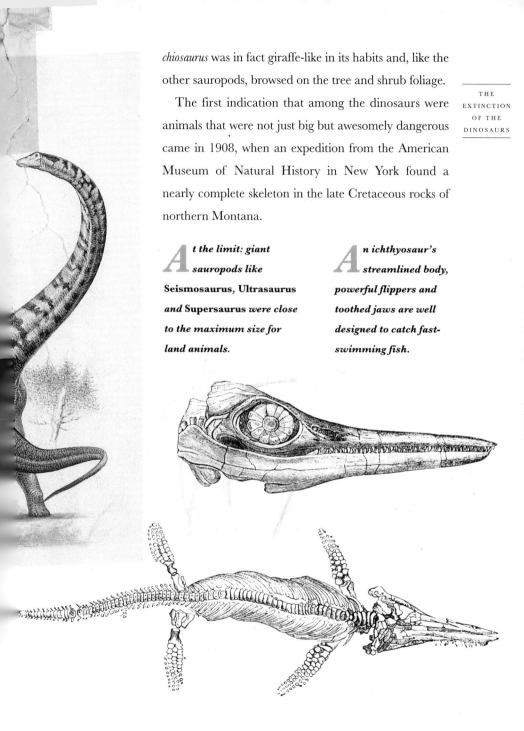

chiosaurus was in fact giraffe-like in its habits and, like the other sauropods, browsed on the tree and shrub foliage.

The first indication that among the dinosaurs were animals that were not just big but awesomely dangerous came in 1908, when an expedition from the American Museum of Natural History in New York found a nearly complete skeleton in the late Cretaceous rocks of northern Montana.

At the limit: giant sauropods like **Seismosaurus, Ultrasaurus** *and* **Supersaurus** *were close to the maximum size for land animals.*

An ichthyosaur's streamlined body, powerful flippers and toothed jaws are well designed to catch fast-swimming fish.

Of all the dinosaurs to have captured the public imagination, the new beast, the giant bipedal carnivore *Tyrannosaurus rex*, has come to epitomize all that is mean and nasty in 'dino-lore'. Standing some 14 m high and weighing around 6 tonnes, with a fine set of 20 cm long carving knives in its jaws, *T. rex* was something special. No modern land-living carnivore comes anywhere near this size. The teeth are designed for one thing only – meat eating. The mystery of *T. rex* relates to the question of whether it could have been an active hunter that ran down, seized and killed its own prey, as it is generally portrayed as doing.

The problem is that tyrannosaurs had extraordinarily small arms, which could not have played any role in capturing or holding prey. Furthermore, calculations show that a beast this size and weight could not have run any faster than about 12 km per hour. If *T. rex* tripped, its arms would not have been able to break the fall and the force of impact would have broken its massive skull. So, it is more likely that that the

***K**ing of the Beasts. The popular image of the dinosaurs was transformed by the discovery of the giant carnivore **Tyrannosaurus rex**.*

tyrannosaurids were scavengers, seeking out kills made by other smaller and more active carnivorous dinosaurs.

There is a considerable mystery about dinosaur reproduction and growth. Like most reptiles dinosaurs laid eggs; the question is, how big would the egg of a 50 tonne, 30 m long dinosaur have been? Using birds as a model and scaling

up from a chicken to an ostrich and on to a large dinosaur, produces the absurdity of a dinosaur egg the size and weight of a small car. Living reptiles, however, such as large crocodiles, which can weigh up to one tonne, lay eggs about the size of a billiard ball, which is relatively small in relation to their body weight. On this scale, the egg of a 50-tonne dinosaur would still be about 20 kg. So far, the largest dinosaur eggs to be found have a weight of no more than 6 kg but are remarkably elongated. A baby curled inside such an egg, would be over a

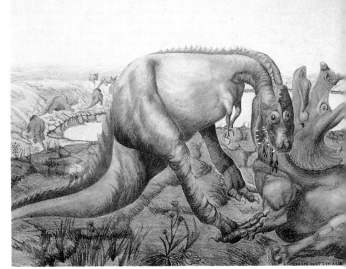

*T**he metre-long skull of the predator* **Allosaurus** *was reduced to* **a bony scaffold for strength and lightness.**

*R**ed in tooth and claw: today, dinosaurs like* **Tyrannosaurus** *have assumed* **the killer image of the legendary dragons.**

metre in length on hatching, which is still very small compared with its 30 m mother. With such a size discrepancy, it is unlikely that its mother could look after the baby and its numerous siblings. These babies must have been capable of fending for themselves almost as soon as they were hatched, just as turtles are.

However, smaller dinosaurs probably had other breeding strategies that required more parental care. Since 1922 and the first discovery of dinosaur nests and eggs in Mongolia it has been evident that at least some dinosaurs lived in social groups and may have cared for their young just as crocodiles do today.

*M*aiasaur *(good mother lizard) nests and eggs show that some dinosaurs looked after their young like most birds do.*

Dino Demise

The mystery of the disappearance of the dinosaurs has taxed scientists for many years now and hundreds of different theories have been put forward to explain what happened to them. Most of these ideas range from the ridiculous to the unlikely, and include death by viral infection, food poisoning, laying eggs with shells too thick for the babies to break out of and producing progeny of

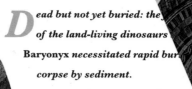

Dead but not yet buried: the *of the land-living dinosaurs* **Baryonyx** *necessitated rapid bur* *corpse by sediment.*

only one sex. Yet some of these theories are not as crazy as they might at first seem. It is known that the sex of crocodile hatchlings is partly determined by the temperature at which they incubate in the nest; global climate change might have done the same for the dinosaurs. Of one thing there is no doubt, the scaly-skinned dinosaurs did die out some 65 million years ago. However, their end is not conveniently marked in the rocks by a global fossil grave-yard, stacked full of bones, with dated headstones.

One of the problems is that there are not enough dinosaur fossils to test an enforced extinction theory against that of gradual decline and disappearance. By late Cretaceous times there were only about 50 kinds of dinosaurs left. By comparison, sea life was much more abundant, with many fossils to be found in the marine rock record. Here, the change from Cretaceous to Tertiary times, which coincides with the extinction event, is well marked by a thin layer of sediment. The layer contains good evidence of a meteorite impact; there is a chemical signature and tiny glass beads of fused rock, which were blown into the atmosphere.

A major meteorite impact should leave a distinctly large crater. After much searching, an appropriately large crater, over 200 km wide, has now been

*R*epositioning **Diplodocus**: *research shows that giant sauropod tails were counterbalance structures, stiffer than previously thought, and did not drag on the ground.*

found at Chicxulub, in the Yucatan peninsula, Mexico, and it seems to be about the right age. Scientists are working to date the impact as accurately as possible. They imagine that the impact threw so much dust into the atmosphere that global temperatures dropped far enough seriously to disturb ecosystems at sea and on land. It follows that any related extinction should be post-impact.

The marine fossil evidence provides the best timing of the event and measure of its impact. Some common fossil micro-organisms suffered a 70 per cent loss of species, but the detailed distribution across the boundary shows that their decline began before the meteorite impact and continued after it. The rocks also show that there was a global fall in sea level and change in ocean circulation patterns at this time. Such changes might not have quite the same media appeal as a meteorite impact, but they are known to have a dramatic effect on life. Around 250 million years ago another even bigger environmental change wiped out 65 per cent of all life forms on Earth without the assistance of any extraterrestrial bodies.

There undoubtedly was a major impact event. The scaly-skinned dinosaurs and their distant marine and flying reptilian relatives did die out, but the last known occurrences of their fossils seem to show that extinction started before the impact. At the moment, the balance of evidence indicates that a meteorite applied the final *coup de grace* to an already declining group of animals caught up in a global phase of environmental change that originated in the oceans.

Dinosaurs Take Off?

It might seem that our metaphor is accurate, and that the dinosaurs became a 'bunch of old fossils' consigned to the dustbin of prehistory, but that is not altogether accurate because the dinosaurs have not entirely gone. In one sense they are still very much with us, it is just that they are now covered in feathers and we call them birds. But it was not a simple matter of the dinosaurs handing

*T*he end is nigh: whilst dinosaurs and
their relatives 'argued', the world
and evolution moved on.

over the baton just as they
crossed the line in the great
evolutionary relay race.

The oldest fossil bird, *Archaeopteryx*, evolved some 150 million years ago. Its skeleton clearly relates the bird to the dinosaurs. The dinosaurs had taken off. It could be argued that the avian dinosaurs are even more successful than their extinct cousins. After all, with around 9,000 different species today, the birds are more successful than mammals, of which there are only some 4,000 species.

Archaeopteryx has a skeleton remarkably similar to a group of small bipedal dinosaurs called the theropods; it is quite possible also that feathers evolved from reptilian scales, because they are made of similar biological ingredients. One big difference between birds and reptiles is that birds are warm-blooded. If birds evolved from dinosaurs, does this mean that dinosaurs were warm-

blooded as well? And, if so, were they all warm-blooded? And anyway how could we tell from the fossils? Major questions like this remain to be answered and are part of the 'life-blood' of dinosaur studies and the continuing fascination of dinosaurs.

Understanding the cause of the extinction of the dinosaurs is not just a matter of scientific curiosity. The fossil remains of past life tell us that the history of life on Earth has been full of such dramatic changes of fortune. Whole

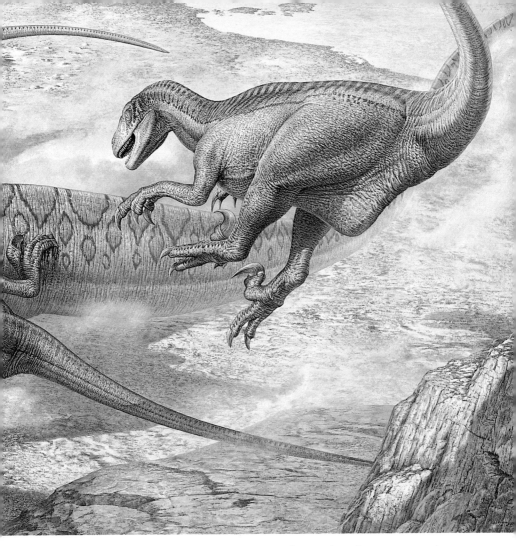

*Co-operative killers: working together, a pack of **Deinonychus** predators could have brought down large prey like this **Tenontosaurus**.*

groups of organisms have come and gone through natural causes completely beyond their control. The geological record shows that climate has always changed and that humans will have to adapt to future change in order to survive. The more that is known about how extinctions happen the better – unless we want to follow the dinosaurs into oblivion.

PHOTOGRAPHIC ACKNOWLEDGEMENTS
Cover The Natural History Museum, London
[NHM]; p. 3 NHM; p. 4 Zefa; pp. 6–7 Oxford
University Museum; pp. 8–9t, 8b NHM;
p. 10 Imitor/P.J. Green [I/PJG];
pp. 11, 12–13 NHM; pp. 14–15 Fortean Picture
Library [FPL]; pp. 16t, 16b I/PJG;
pp. 16–17, 18–19 Mary Evans Picture Library
[ME]; p. 20 [I/PJG; p. 21 NHM; p. 23 I/PJG;
p. 24 NHM; p. 25t FPL; pp. 26, 28 NHM;
p. 29 ME; pp. 30–31, 32–3, 34–5 NHM;
p. 37 FPL; pp. 38–9 NHM.

THE
EXTINCTION
OF THE
DINOSAURS

First published in Great Britain 1997
by George Weidenfeld and Nicolson Ltd
The Orion Publishing Group
5 Upper St Martin's Lane
London WC2H 9EA

Text copyright © Douglas Palmer, 1997
The moral right of the author has been asserted
Design and layout copyright © George Weidenfeld
and Nicolson Ltd, 1997

A CIP catalogue record for this book is available
from the British Library
ISBN 0 297 823140

Picture Research: Suzanne Williams

Designed by Harry Green

Typeset in Baskerville

First published 2002

Daabacaaddii 2aad / Second edition 2004.

Halabuur Communications
PO Box 43446
LONDONSE11 4YW
United Kingdom
Email: halabuur@aol.com

Waxaa lagu daabacay Ingiriiska.

Printed and bound in Great Britain

ISBN 0-9545165-0-8

DAL DAD WAAYEY
iyo
DUNI DAMIIR BEESHAY

Soomaaliya Dib Ma u Dhalan doontaa?

**A Land without Leaders in a
World without Conscience: Can Somalia be
Resurrected?**

**Daabacaad 2aad
La sii tifaftiray**

Maxamed Daahir Afrax

Halabuur Communications
London